BREATHING IN, BREATHING OUT

This book is for Jerry

The Philip Levine Prize for Poetry is an annual prize sponsored by the M.F.A. Program in Creative Writing at California State University, Fresno. This prize was initiated in 2001 to honor Philip Levine — who taught in Fresno for many years, and is one of the great American poets of the twentieth century — and to provide a book-publishing venue for a worthy American poet. Each year the M.F.A. Program awards the Levine Prize to the author of the best original, unpublished book-length manuscript of poetry entered in our competition. We are proud to join in partnership with Anhinga Press as the publisher and distributor of our prize-winning volumes.

CONTENTS

IV. WORD

V. SILENCE

ACKNOWLEDGMENTS

Thanks to the following periodicals in which
these poems first appeared:

Alaska Quarterly Review, "Leaving Lewisburg on Easter Morning"

Ariel, "The Hare and the Tortoise"

Georgia Review, "Your Body"

Indiana Review, "Kitten"

Iowa Review, "Mary Rose Quotes James Joyce on the Cliffs at Bray"

Michigan Quarterly Review, "Buying the King-sized Bed, "Impatiens"

Midwest Quarterly, "Why We Plan to Move"

Poetry, "The Pupil," "Monarchs," "Highway 5"

Prairie Schooner, "Chicken Bone," "Rumors of Changes," "Somewhere"

Shenandoah, "Sunday Morning," "For the Inauguration of William Jefferson Clinton, 1997," "Samantha Quits Growing"

The Southern Review, "Hyperspace," "Amy and Brian," "I Write My Mother a Poem"

Tar River Review, "Chat"

West Branch, "Language"

Yarrow, "Cosmic Pitching," "Dogs"

"Kitten" is reprinted in *Writing Poems, 4th ed.,* ed. Robert Wallace and Michelle Boisseau. "The Pupil" is reprinted in the *Anthology of Magazine Verse and Yearbook of American Poetry,* ed. Alan Pater, Palm Springs, CA: Monitor. "Einstein on Mercer Street" was performed as a piece for orchestra and voice by the Pittsburgh New Music Ensemble in 2002.

I am grateful to the University of Delaware for a Fellowship in the Center for Advanced Studies which enabled me to finish this book. My deep thanks, also, to Jeanne Murray Walker, with whom I've worked on poems for over twenty years, and to Julianna Baggott and David Scott. It was a great pleasure to collaborate with Kevin Puts, the composer of the musical score for the Einstein poems, by phone and e-mail during his year in Italy as winner of the 2002 Rome Prize and, simultaneously, a Guggenheim Fellowship in musical composition. I wish also to thank Melinda Putz, who suggested Einstein to us as a subject. I am also grateful to Andrea Hollander Budy for her invaluable help with revisions of the Einstein poem. And finally, to Lynne Knight, my gratitude and admiration for the care with which she edited and designed this book.

BREATHING IN, BREATHING OUT

True singing is a different kind of breath.
A breath about nothing. A blowing in the god. A wind.
Rilke, *The Sonnets to Orpheus, I, 3*

Coming and going, we never leave home.
The Diamond Sutra

I.

AIR

FOURTH OF JULY PARADE, ALBION, WA.

Everyone's happy, catching candy.
There's an army truck; one fire truck
screaming; a blue Olds about 1975;
two police cars side by side,
everything huzza-huzza,
the band playing "From the Halls of Montezuma"
from a flatbed truck; eight kids on bikes,
with balloons; a dozen 4-H kids in clover-shirts;
a bulldog with a bow;
two hefty rodeo girls on horses,
a small tractor pulling prizewinning chickens
in their two festooned cages.
I can't help it, I get sentimental tears.
Damn, I say to myself. Chickens.
A prize for being chickens.

Then, amazingly, here they all come again,
back up the street, chickens
from the other side,
fiddle-players instead of horns showing,
candy flying again like stars.
Everything a copy of itself, another chance.
Quantum physics says it's true,
particles coming and going.
The road not taken may be taken.
Meanwhile, the chickens move forward
again in our eyes, the Declaration of Independence
gets signed. We need custom,
return. We like to sit sandal-footed in the grass,
happily surrendered to either side.
Past or future, it's no wonder
the chickens win, the way they keep
their artist's eyes cocked, lost in the work
of being chickens
　　　　　again and again.

BUYING THE KING-SIZED BED

I'm already thinking of rolling around that expanse,
tossing a leg without entangling. The way I am,

though, I see all the possibilities for loss. I see us
pillowed and billowed, supported in exactly the right

hollows by ergonomically designed, pocketed coils,
while beneath it all — the pea under a royal height —

the oppressed, the downsmashed, sleep in despoiled
cardboard boxes, or three on one frayed blanket.

Think of us, spread out, tongues on the rampage,
marking where we'll kiss. Oh wild God, how can

you permit this excess? How could any of us gauge
the exact distance at which people turn strangers

to each other? In our double bed — called double,
but we have been bumper-cars and cliff hangers

on it for years, our shorter ancestors troubling
us still — I can't even raise my knee

without poking my dear love in the groin.
We have been close, we have understood each other

the way people in tight houses start growing
together — at a molecular level, absorbing

each other's pheromones. Yelling and slamming doors,
too, or else they are lost inside each other! They would

have grand houses, if they could. They would forge
on like jet-skis through the foyer and out to the good

sea. They would send a wire to say, "I still
love you." The sweet old world is longing to be

loose and light. All night long it stares up at the chilled
stars. This is a sticky business, finding the peak

distance for love, knowing our bodies will be nothing,
someday, wanting to hear them make their delicious,

reassuring sounds, bobbing against each other.

COSMIC PITCHING

Fydrich would lift his wild golden curls
and talk to the sky. Hrabosky the same,
and he'd talk to the ball, circling
the mound, face twitching. And then he would
face the centerfield fence, whirl back
around, go into his stretch, and
pitch.

      It's best not to take chances. You
get your mind stalking and empty.
You slap your glove on your thigh, pace
your pattern. You make a ring of not-caring
around the thing. Too much pressure on one
point and the energy's down a black hole.
Carlton, on the watch for UFOs, what he might
have been doing is picking up an
archipelago as it moved through its
calculations. His mind was just breathing
in and out.

           So much that's far-fetched
lodges between the in and the out.
Did I mention Luis Tiant, flinging his
head to the sky as his arm came down?
Proof that the center of the world is in
the body, not the sight. You get these actions
together that don't care about each other.
They don't stand for anything.
                Listen, ball.
Bless you, ball. You and I, ball.
You get into a rhythm. Inside the rhythm
is a pitch. You keep your mind on the
rhythm, waiting to feel the pitch coming on.
You don't know how to speak directly to
the thing you want more than anything.

SOMEWHERE

I am all right. Everyone else is out there
crying and going on, but I have gotten
in here with my nice dead grandmother.
They have her on a gurney, legs
sticking out of the sheet, the red stem
from her thigh to the canister
on the floor.

     Getting her ready for the
funeral, honey, taking the blood out.
We're going to put this clear stuff in
before she's cold, so she'll be beautiful.
Already she is, clean as stone.
I am all right here. I am happy
enough in her little room with the
smells, even after the scrubbing.

   My hand on her arm, so they
have to say *dead* again, and they say it
exactly the way I knew it, something you
check out and pass on by, dead
robin, dead rabbit, dead worm, nothing
to turn back for but a kiss
on her mouth, which is flat.
   She can't feel that, the one in
suspenders says, *but somewhere, she knows.*

Somewhere begins separating itself,
stretching itself into the field
behind the house, into the tall
grass, the things to be found
in it — the mole holes to China, the zillion
little stone eyes of Africa turned up

to me. I am holding my
breath between continents, while she lies
pinned to the center, wearing
her glasses. If I stretch out my hand,
the air is a faceless body
and I am standing here
like a dumb bunny with my hand, pulling
it back into my memory.

KITTEN

She is thirteen. Her cat, Sneakers,
has just had another litter of kittens
to be chloroformed by her father
in the large cooking pot. "Keep whichever
you want," he says, "mother or kitten,
just one." She is sitting on her bed
petting the male kitten with thick
tan fur. She sits close to her Silvertone
radio, moves her mouth to the music.
A rifle cracks in the back yard,
then a scuffle like a rat
under the house. Sneakers has gotten
away, not quite dead, is crouched
in a far corner wailing a low
steady wail. She watches the square
knob on her dresser, lit with sun,
the back hairs of her kitten ablaze
in the sunlight like little spines.
Under her is the live crawlspace.
She holds the little paws of her kitten,
pushes her thumbs gently into the center
of the pads with almost divine
tenderness, watches the claws extend
involuntarily, translucent little hooks.
She has a vision of pushing until they fly
outward like darts, or rays of sun,
leaving the kitten with buff-
colored buttons of feet. She names it
Buffy, imagines buffing the DeSoto
with the kitten, rubbing him flat
as her grandmother's fox stole,
popping in little marbles for eyes

that would catch the light,
hard. Her father is calling kitty, here
kitty, his flashlight in the cat's
eyes. It is Jungle-Cat, leaping out
of a 3-D screen among arrows, flying
at the audience. She stretches out on
the bed and brushes her face across
her smooth animal. A dark creature passes
through the back chambers of her thought
like a shadow, enters a kingdom
of shadows, stirring and stirring.

LEWIS THE INDOOR CAT

To have it all mapped out, upstairs bedroom for morning sun,
sofa in the afternoon, wild chasing
of the mouse-toy at night,
the eye of the world shut again.

The deep grip of waiting, kitchen smells blooming and fading.

From a vast height, the desperate ant.

Why should he turn? Who could ever add it up?

You can hear them, the shrill cheeps, the cawing of what can't be reached.
The day staring in with its huge eyes.

The world inhales and exhales its humans.
So, he is running to the top of the stairs, turning on his back
to have his stomach rubbed, scouring the hand
that rubs him, scouring his paws
as if he could start at the fur-tips of himself and take it all in.

The actual life of Lewis, all that can be found in it,
the couch matted with hairs, the stairs to be sat on,
and meowed on, one by one.

The crossing and recrossing from room to room,
the sense of what is ceasing and beginning
rolling like waves through his thinking.

The constant reference to the closet where the food is kept,
the hope that feels like an immense intelligence.

HIGHWAY 5

We take the direct shot
instead of the coastal route,
not being able to have
everything, of course.
None of that entanglement:
fantastical ruffling of bays
and inlets, little houses
with slammed doors, gravel
driveways, faces with
three-days' growth of beard.
This bleached line singing
like an aria, not part of
the general narrative.
Like a neutrino, beamed
through everything without
flinching. Ah, to travel
light as light, to hold to
the straight and narrow idea,
to take the wheel and —
as if it were a museum
cross section of a giant redwood —
draw a straight line
from its center: "Magna Carta
Signed. Columbus Discovers
America. Civil War Begins."
There goes our personal
will, petty prejudices
elegantly tossed off behind
like Isadora's scarf.
There goes this difficult language
dashing like wild horses
into its heaven of metaphor.

Where we're headed, the setting
sun's a long-stemmed rose
held out before the 18-
wheelers: THE END, backlit
pink, a campfire in the dark.

THE POET LAUREATE ADDRESSES
THE DELAWARE LEGISLATURE OPENING
ITS FIRST SESSION AFTER SEPTEMBER 11

Naturally we go on, even though the great
double watermark stands behind everything, now.

Even this poem — if you held it to the light,
you could see the Towers shadowing behind it, their steel

beams bare couplets of moonlight. How free
this poem might have been, I like to imagine,

if the Towers hadn't shaped it. How free the air was,
before its division into good and evil, before

the planes, before the law of gravity. What law
could we possibly have passed to keep the air from leaning

one way instead of the other? Here we are,
in Delaware, a breath south of New York: whatever

shadows the City, surely shadows us.
And, too, we have these eroding beaches, poultry

manure greening the bay, houses spreading
across the broad expanse of farms. Still,

here comes this poem, setting up its boundaries,
its own little rules, trying to start over, to be

the kind of poem even kids can say by heart.
It wants St. Georges bridge in it, arched like a dolphin,

the C & D canal gleaming through it like a crack
in an egg lit from the inside. It wants to be the kind

of poem with snow geese lifting off from Bombay Hook.
Word by word it starts building itself out of nothing.

It listens to its heart, the encouraging beat of its heart's
own law, law, law — except for

that double shadow, that one missed systole,
diastole — and then again the blessed law.

II.

WATER

RUMORS OF CHANGES

On the island, you have at least
Dostoyevsky, the Bible,

and penguins, a trembling sea
of penguins, an ice-floe of waddle,

alert in their water of thoughts.
It is an island of flat-footed

parents and children
caressing each other with their

noses, playing at likeness and un-
likeness. They angle across

the ice the way I do across this
page, dear one, a little wavery

from the tears in my eyes.
Things will change, I write

to you. Look at the way your grief's
in motion already, a little island

of sociability. I am awkward
writing it, but I keep hoping to

build momentum, get the words
to start blackening the shoreline.

And don't you have
the classics, sort of a general

history? And the penguins,
all cocking their heads as if the

air were magnetized? You could
watch the way they try to catch

which sounds they should
turn to, in the circus of sounds.

SUNDAY MORNING

They are miles out in the country, so you will have to
imagine them at the glass-topped table, having their oatmeal,

watching the awful house-finches fight at the feeder, squirrels
gathering up the scattered seed. She tells him about the copper-

age Iceman in *National Geographic*, the oldest intact human,
5,000 years old, dug out of snow in the Italian Alps. She describes

his body, lean as a jackal, flesh sucked against the bone, his
face dark and a little moldy but still entirely covered by skin.

"He looked tense on the snow," she says, "his hip torn by a
jackhammer, his genitals broken away." They watch the finches.

Her husband asks about the jackhammer, and the genitals.
"It was a policeman who did it," she answers, "thinking he had

a newly dead man to pull out." They talk about the blundering
human race, as people do in the complacency of oatmeal and

oranges, before they start their day. The husband is thinking
about his Baptist childhood, the sin of the world placed on his

small heart, and the Iceman's hip crushed like a bird's
wing. He wishes the Iceman had been left under the glacier

holding his precious packet of cells. "They're afraid of
being alone. That's why they dug him up," the wife says, slicing

her orange. "We keep longing to find our old selves still under
the ice while we've gone on inventing cars and airplanes."

"But what will happen to him now?" he asks. "Behind glass,"
she replies. Their separate thoughts converge at the glass

and look in. The woods are bright as glass, after the rain.
The closer they look, the more the copper-age man breaks up,

like a newspaper photograph at close range. In town, other
people are at church, singing hymns. If you could get to a point

as high as God, the man, the woman, and the congregation
would turn into dots, just the same. You would miss the wife's

hand coming to rest on the husband's knee like a blessing.

COW FALLING

*There is a story of the crew of a Japanese fishing trawler picked up at
sea, who claimed their boat had been sunk by a cow falling out of the
sky. It turns out they weren't drunk. Russian soldiers had stolen a cow
out of a field and for a prank had loaded it on their transport plane to
take back to Russia. But the terrified cow dashed madly back and
forth, banging into the walls of the hold until they decided for their
own safety, they had better push it out over the sea.*

The cow that jumped over the moon
drifts now like a table down —
not drifting, really, but ripping along as if she had been shot
from one of Monty Python's catapults, hysterical bulk,
udder waving in so much brooding space
she appears to drift
toward a rippling plain below.
As the sun strikes her, she lights up, a Golden Calf now,
an astrological sign, an advertisement — Elsie the Cow —
if the fishermen would look up.
But they are preparing the trawler like a manger for the event,
coiling ropes, pulling in nets.
They are passing over the surface, oblivious
as the clipper in Breugel's painting,
while the heavens are opening,
while the cow lists temporarily to the side, feels the sag
of her body, watches the only sky available
in the last, interesting minutes —
though it is all the same, clouds or plains of water,
rolling across her vast mind.
Now she herself is rolling for no reason back to her feet
above the widening black craft where the Japanese fishermen
are hauling the last net in, laughing
in their small brotherhood of hunger and smells.
The cow falls heavy, and heavy,
monotonous and unromantic, part of all things falling in nature.

At the last second they see her as she sees them,
each uselessly drawing back in mute recognition
before the shattering, the counter-idea,
which is definitely wrong in one sense and regrettable,
which could be, though, exactly what the gods intended,
another unusual birth and death
of a few moments' duration, to be believed or not,
an ancient Chinese koan
to drive the thinking mind out of itself
to rest on the fluctuating sea.

SPRING

As soon as I start to pay strict attention
        to that white lily diving upwards
like a ballerina, naturally

I look up and there's a man on the trestle,
        studying the murky water.
I have no way to gauge

the exact depth of his misery. Maybe
        he's thinking of jumping.
I could be recalling yesterday's Oprah show

about the man who jumped
        and only one guy in a whole crowd
tried to save him,

too late. Though when I see him there,
        even in my imagination,
I wonder if it's my ex-husband, always

on the edge of a cliff or a trestle,
        smoking a Tareyton, thinking he'll
jump. How no one could save him,

but my brain keeps ledges he can quietly
        sit on for a while.
This is what I'm used to: the one thing

like the sweet uplifted arms of the lily,
        and then the other. Neither speaks
to the other; there's not much to say.

They could be dancing the Tango,
 eyes outward into space,
moving as if the other's only something to

maneuver with, to keep things going.
 But it's Spring, so
let's say the man on the trestle's remembering

his daughter's twelfth birthday,
 when she asked him to dance with her
in her new ballerina slippers.

When I said "ballerina," in reference to
 the lily, he thought, instead,
of her skinny beauty, before she took the job

at Burger King and gained the weight
 and moved in with her boyfriend,
although these days he feels lighter,

released from her life a little.
 And she's going on a diet, quitting
smoking. This is what spring is like.

In the grass by the lily, a worm's
 probably opening little breathing tubes
in the earth. The man can

sit up there all day, breathing. He can keep on
 looking like a leftover hippie,
pulling down his dirty Dodgers' cap.

He can keep on, without me.

LEAVING LEWISBURG ON EASTER MORNING

Under clouds, the Juniata River's pewter,
pitted with eddies like an old mirror.
I'm zipping along
thinking of a person's reflection
worn away. I don't like to keep
saying goodbye, with all this moisture
and springtime. The churches are looking
upward and downward, but I am thinking of
how fast insects fly, how they create
their own vortex of air like a tiny tornado,
always on the edge of stalling out,
but they don't, because the outer tip
of the wings moves faster and throws air off
the end. Very ingenious.
Horseflies can copulate
in the air at ninety miles per hour.

Probably things that seem mysterious
have simple explanations involving
engineering, luminous and metallic
as the Juniata. I drive alongside the river
almost to Harrisburg,
thinking now of huge gray catfish
underneath mopping their whiskers
against the mud, creating their own map.
And then a line gets pulled, the fins open out
like kites, the mouth gapes like a huge
bottle-opener! It may turn out to be nothing
up there but one small johnboat, a simple
period. But suppose that period
were an insect, with oars for wings
and could take me anywhere.
I wouldn't want to leave for another world,

but keep on straight along this one,
that would turn out cleverly
to be everywhere I go.

III.

SUN

MONARCHS

The monarchs blink
along the buddlia bush, eye-level, acting like
the butterflies of my childhood, except
for the one that fights its way
to the top of the poplar tree.
All of them, though, are starting to agitate

over their upcoming trip to Venezuela —
who would have thought it? — little torqued-up
leather-wings, miniature thrusts,
as if someone had dropped
a Picasso and made monarchs, splintered
into Monet or Manet,

thousands of jewels —
diamonds — because a butterfly's wings
have no pigment at all,
only prisms that try to deflect attention
from the fiercely secret source.
Easy to imagine that one thing stands for another:

monarchs erupting
wet from a former life, baptised by immersion.
Forgive me, I only recently learned
they have no former life. The caterpillar melts
down to pure DNA. It is not a matter of reshaping,
as if it had a sex-change operation. It is

a monarch, finally
shed of whatever sluggish thoughts
had dramatically misunderstood what life this is.

FEET

The private pains burrow into you like troglodytes.
Take my feet: on the treadmill I try to pretend
they never touch base on the push-offs. This flies
for a while. Still, it's the same feet intended

for saddle oxfords forever, the same feet
that eventually fanned out like dead angels, bones
flat on the floor. Suppose there's no seat
at a cocktail party: I can decide to talk of Plato

for maybe thirty minutes before it all
comes down to feet. Sometimes I curse the footloose.
Sometimes, though, I recognize the funereal
man at Goodwill sorting clothes, the snoot

of his big toe poking out like a ripe olive
from a hole cut in his shoe, and I'm one
with the world. When I'm sitting on the solid
couch, as now, rubbing one sole with my thumb,

the pain is like a secret between us, a fortissimo
of pleasure: us against the world. Sometimes
I plant clover blooms between my toes
on a summer day. They line up clever as rhymes,

or little purple votive candles, dispersed
like four prayers out of the cracks of the earth.

DOGS

I am off for my walk along the shore,
a cold and windy day like the one Elizabeth Bishop wrote about

in "The End of March," the sky the same mutton-fat jade,
even if I don't know what mutton-fat looks like.

I remember she was following dog-prints big as lion-prints.
The biggest dog here is Josie, more like a barge

than a lion. She limps arthritically up the street,
eternally optimistic. Amanda and Dewey disband their symposium

so everyone can kiss each other in secret places.
Then the lab with the red bandana comes up.

Then I come to the three full-sized poodles, teeth bared.
The white one has gotten out of her fence and starts

after me, red bows bobbing over her ears.
I don't know why I can't just walk down the road thinking

about how Elizabeth Bishop turns her sun into a stalking lion.
Probably it was a shadow. I feel a little responsible

for the animals, I pet them when they let me.
I do it in memory of my poor brother, and Mrs. Laverty,

who taught him the 300 words before he died, and I do it
in memory of the yelling and sobbing. I could just as well do it

for Elizabeth Bishop, opening her eyes, trying to remember
what to be ashamed of, how many words

betrayed by drink. I try to remember her poem, the animals
shadowing me, stammering and practicing,

breaking my heart with what they can't say.
Their faces are like boarded-up summer houses, canny

but withdrawn. When I look at them directly, whichever dogs
have come along, dubiously nose the ground. And sometimes

I wonder if they should trust me at all, the way I get lost
in Bishop and her lion and mutton-fat jade

while the world around me is
slurping and sniffing with recognition and pleasure.

IMPATIENS

You start some in pots,
      set some six inches apart
         in beds, red
and pink. You want them to hurry
      and join together,
         all flowers, without
the mulch. There is nothing
      to say because
         they are working
as hard as they can, coming on
      delicately, fluttering
         their flat faces
in the breeze. For weeks
      there will be space
         and a few blooms.
Then blooms only, a pleasure
      free of you, floating
         a little above ground
as if someone were rubbing
      your back with the faintest
         fingertips.
You feel your spine relax,
      your whole body
         one gesture
headed earthward,
      away from your mind,
         away from
your personal idea of heaven,
      toward the blossom
         of light.

MARY ROSE QUOTES JAMES JOYCE
ON THE CLIFFS AT BRAY

We are chuffing along in our heavy shoes,
watching a scene on a nearby peak:
"She's sitting on his hips, now,

running her hands up and down his chest,"
Mary Rose says, as if I couldn't see, myself.
Martello tower's across, and the house

of that terrible Christmas dinner
in *Portrait of the Artist*. Mary Rose quotes
the beginning: "Once upon a time, and a very

good time it was." We recall what followed,
the tears for poor, dead Parnell,
for the abused stones of Ireland, the very same

stones that young woman braces her feet on,
now, as if to say, "What of it?"
Here we are, clumping upward, across

from the pearl-pale seemingly quenchless lovers,
seaweed masses rocking below.
It all feels out of hand: Joyce's Christmas

gone haywire, politics tangled with the mother's
breast, the breast of turkey, the wine,
and now this ecstasy near enough to touch,

the whole universal exclamation thrown upward
out of the mind. "I could never, there,"
Mary Rose says, and I agree,

but the scene is working in us, a pebble
in the shoe. From the beginning, sure,
we had hoped to be loved without conditions

until we cried out among the seagulls.
We are quiet now, we know exactly
what we are up to, we are busily wrapping

the lovers in layers and layers of language.

BURREN

We pull off the road
to walk the plains of rock,
the moonscape of the Burren.

Think of the painful effort required
to make something out of nothing, the point
at which you imagine it trying
to rise, but you don't know what it is,
except it is awful and hopeless.

Speak through my mouth, my speech, you tell it.

In the interstices —
deep pools, little tropical gardens.
Someone has made three small stone altars
over three pools. Kids,

maybe, who found the old coins
and key rings at the bottom during a dry season
and added green and blue perfume bottles,
a white elf figurine on top.

It might have been winter.
They might have pretended they were on an iceberg.

They laid things out on the rock.
It began to look like a little city,
the one they'll get to the minute they can drive,
where the stone will open its eyes
and see what a hard time they've had, coping
with this barren life.

HYPERSPACE

Tree trunks seem to keep shrinking all winter,
and by mid-March the Elk River's visible in blips

from horizon to horizon, when the sun's going
down. Some things I want, I only get a glimpse

of. Coltrane at his gentlest — you can still hear
what's harnessed, though. He might be playing "Soul Eyes,"

but it's not just eyes. His sax is opening its
mouth like a hole in space. I have the theory of a

net laid across as a kind of protection. It is like
latitude and longitude, or more abstractly, the warp

and woof of belief, the kind of thinking that
separates day from night, heaven from earth, and so on.

Suppose the universe began as a tear in the fabric
of another universe. On a two-dimensional plane,

the tear would look like a pushed-out curve
the shape of Coltrane's saxophone. What if there are

ten dimensions, and Coltrane is in the three
of space and the one of time, and the rest are hidden?

They might be quivering out there like branches
of invisible trees, or wormholes in the branches. This

is a very religious feeling, beyond belief. Not
everything is vertical or horizontal. I keep thinking

I should do something instead of just stand
here, it is all so beautiful for the few minutes

I can see the flat plane of blazing water
through the trees, and the terrific sun on the brink.

IV.

WORD

LANGUAGE

One day Adam said "Adam"
and found out he was standing

across the field from everything
else. It scared him half to death.

He lifted his arms as if they
could help. The air felt cool.

So he said "air" and "cool":
a population of not-Adams

sprouted everywhere. One
of them was Eve, a wild card.

He heard her clearly, distinct
from his internal voice, his

private naming. She was singing
"In time, the Rockies may crumble,

Gibraltar may tumble …"
and sure enough, it was

something o'clock already.
He saw that her mouth was pink.

"Pink," he said, because it was
small and had lips to push the air

away. And there was something
else, he was sure of it, a softening

of the air between them,
a spell. Nothing could be the word

for it. He was reeling
with the wound of it, the chink

between subject and object.
Light entered, memory followed

and began to tell its own story.
He felt himself held in it,

traveling *within* it, now,
driving toward a particular town.

"Something's happened,"
he said to her, but she'd guessed

the doom of it already, the wooden
signs along the highway

bravely standing for everything
that matters: *Burma Shave,*

*Kollectibles Kottage, The Cock
& Bull.* She ran a finger delicately

along the window as if she could
trace what it was that had

broken loose from the two
of them, that was running crazy

out there, never looking back.

CHAT

The absence of chat bothers me
every winter. If one word can get away
like that, I begin doubting everything.
I used to try to get to the library in Fayetteville,
grinding chat under my feet up Dickson street
(trying to get to the real library, not the bar
by the same name), and that was definitely
chat heaped against the snowbank.
Small particles disappear, then it's easy
to slip, an armload of books skidding
halfway down the block. I remember
the block where I knew all the names: Bauder,
Glenn, Adams, Craig, Stevens. I know
these were right, before they died. Now
all the rooms have been redecorated.
I wonder if I'm okay. I get the entire
Arkansas Highway Department fixed in my mind,
the men finishing their cigarettes, saying
"Load up that chat, we're spreading chat
today." Chat is poured into trucks.
The men have no idea of the circumference
of their world. They think it goes on forever.
I say *chat* to the people I know here.
They've never heard of it. Things in my past
might not have happened. My first husband
laid his hard hat on the table. I'm not
sure if I was there. I look up *gravel*
in the dictionary. I look up *chat*, which is
only a verb. I feel a little guilty,
filling in where nothing exists. When my
father is talking, I still have to work hard

to get a word in and make it stick.
When my mother is talking,
I have to find a word, put it in her mouth
and let it rattle around so she can make a sound.
I am almost crying, trying to get her to say
anything. I describe the absence the best
I can. A man and a woman are on opposite sides
of the street, calling across. They have had a life
I don't know, I can't even hear them, in my car.
Two trucks in front of me are full of chat.
I take it as a sign I should write this.

WHY WE PLAN TO MOVE

To give us credit, we never
imagined two neighbors with backhoes.
Neighbor One "landscapes" by levering

out his trees. Neighbor Two plows under
the so-called "trash trees" and shrubs "
to "discourage termites." Number One

is going up and down outside
my study window, flattening a wide
swath for a swimming pool or tennis court,

he can't decide. Number Two
is pushing the wilderness abreast
like a street cleaner, as if he possessed

no subconscious. I don't want
to be a bleeding-heart, but it's all day,
up and down, scraping a holiday

out of so much sorrow, as if the earth
were a sullen old sheep and they, being
farm boys, had to try fucking.

Now I'm stuck with that nasty thought,
and what's under it, the raw lining
of the world. Even today, Sunday,

Number One's out there, riding
his speechless ground. And Number Two's
lit a fiery furnace, is lifting

logs on with the concentration of a Puritan,
making his mind repent, again,
from the particular, log by log.

CHICKEN BONE

I can almost see my mother
rolling her eyes, trying to
get her breath, my father
coming behind to do the Heimlich
maneuver in Mrs. Pete's restaurant,
Mrs. Pete herself — she of the
$4.95 dinner, dessert included —
stepping in to do it right.

Before this, what?
They are talking about the heat,
maybe, the grosbeak
on the feeder, the rusting screens.

How long could that go on?
The menu could take a while.
A missing earring.
This is the way they
spend their lives
in our absence, this and
The Young and the Restless.
        "I'm finding out what makes
the young restless,"
he says.
        We children and the soaps,
swarming around their chicken
and mashed potatoes
like starved ghosts,
while they behave politely
to each other, God knows —
charity and violence having closed

together above them like
a little tent at last: the third
thing they've refused to speak
of, the limit to everything.

Guess what they do
now? They figure the tip
on a napkin, not one cent
extra for the life they're in.

AMY AND BRIAN

A freshman at the University of Delaware secretly gave birth at
a local motel, attended by the child's father, also a college
freshman. The newborn was then apparently bludgeoned to
death and its body left in a plastic bag in a dumpster behind
the motel. An autopsy revealed that the child had had a brain
defect, not visually apparent and not fatal, that causes seizures
and mental retardation.
                        — Newark, Delaware, December 1996

We see the yellow Comfort Inn sign, the low run
of rooms in front of the pool, the pool spread with blue

plastic, night air chill on feverish skin —
must be feverish — air overcome with breathing,

two fogged breaths from the Toyota to the corridor
of windows, to the single number. Then the close room:

dresser, mirror, round table, two double beds.
They have brought a diet Coke. They are sitting on the bed,

maneuvering onto the bed. We are out of this, now,
dim room wrapping more and more into itself,

her hands gripping the sheets. Let them then watch
each other, the great transformation opening itself leisurely,

by degrees, between them with no help, her arms
and legs spread now like wings on the bed, watching

each other come to this final opening as if the first
passionate moment had been nothing, only a twinge

of this practical work, the space between them coming
to a single point, not one thought left: perfect,

perfected, driven together into sightlessness, empty,
knowing nothing, spilling toward each other in an ecstasy

of suffering. Let them be urged on and on
into it, toward the crowning head, shock of hair,

shoulders. Let him pull to rescue himself from the pushing;
let her push to rescue herself from the pulling.

Let them be a single unit, local, out of our reach.
Now she is through, split like the Red Sea,

small blood and water cupped under her hips.
And he is Superman, back-lit by the dresser lamp,

holding the child by the head and back, holding it
gently, cord still strung, as if he can never

have enough, now, having seen his molecules put together
into this, into these arms and legs, this thin

cry, this blind thrust that has come so far
on its own. The mother is lifting her head — let her lift

her head, if we could see — legs still spread.
Between her bare legs her innermost dark

broken into light as he holds it, seeing the child
begin to pitch forward, to tremble and seize unnaturally,

proving the disorder, the unnaturalness of this event,
while the others are studying Hegel or Joyce, or walking

across campus within the bubbles of their own laughter.
A whole semester of two people's fixation on one

dread moment has naturally over-excited the brain
into this violent seizure! As if the trouble now freed

is jerked with lightning! It is time to turn back.
To stop the example risen between them of what

they appear to be, to take up again who they surely
still are. She turns her head away, a signal. He shakes

the child to stop the seizure, shakes an insane string
of expletives out of himself, inaccurate and absurd,

as if he has been deeply offended. She puts the pillow
over her own face into the unfolding speechless dream,

everything and nothing at once. Everything the dream
teaches is an empty boat, a limp sail,

while he is shaking. And while she is not looking
he takes the base of the table lamp and pounds, stopping

utterly the possibility of waking. Now we see
the floating debris of the dream, diet Coke, tennis shoes,

bloody sheets, wrinkled shirt, key on the dresser,
two freshmen opening their eyes, putting the child

down on the bed as if it were a finished book.
Now they are ready to step into the glorious past.

She draws the trash bag — Did they bring the bag? Did they
anticipate all this? — over the child,

slides the child down until nothing could be missing
from their lives, shroud of curtains across the new daylight.

Up 896, across College Avenue, their friends
stay inside the brick walls of the campus, a constant

to be relied on, easing to mind, as they do now —
sleeping, or listening to CDs, laughing or talking —

the fabulous fortune of the friends' phrasing. But now
the two are leaving their own bleeding fraction

of the universe, wiping off the lamp and bathroom sink,
flushing soggy tissues. The day tips forward

out the door, holds steady; the bag goes in the bin
behind the rows of rooms — tilts away — off

to the side, among the boxes and other bags, and we
are all gone down and shall be raised out of this

awfulness, raised into our choral outcry, while those two
are borne back into the world, fogged, she bleeding

still, exhausted. Sun's exploding off the cars
as if the cars were suns themselves. Light burns

across their eyes. It may be hard to drive — this is what
we think to say — looking out, however we can.

THE PUPIL

Sometimes she would ask, as a distraction,
"Play the Minute Waltz," and Miss J.
would start a few irritable bars, *accelerando*,

before resuming the pencil tap on
the stacked books, half-notes, quarter-notes:
"No, no, quick-quick sl-o-o-w-ly now,"

her pupil's fingers would lurch behind
the words. "You're wasting your grandmother's
money," Miss J. would quietly say,

part of the lesson, close to the end.
Sometimes Miss J. would want a duet; her pupil
would drop all hope of her own existence,

alternate notes coming on like a great blind train
against her hands, her ears. She would collapse
her hands into the nest of her lap,

collapse her vision to the level of
the yellow cat Miranda, who would edge
behind the metronome's dire heart,

pad to the window to watch through its bars
the talented traffic, twitch her soft ears
to catch the endless rattle and laughter

below. She would settle her amber hips,
turned away from the helpless pupil. Between
the two of them would rest the unpolished

floor, the smell of wood, the private
suffering of the grandly complex and dissonant
soul among the staffs and lances.

The way I keep trying to write
this poem, plodding into words.
First I had a daughter, then a son.
I got married young, I stood
at the top of the stairs, smoking
a cigarette, watching the sun
go down, the frantic starlings.
This was the beginning of what
I think of as grief, my second life
poised, ready to dash off.
      I wanted to mourn for
Jack Kennedy, for my blue
Volkswagen, I wanted to live
in a nicely decorated house,
but I kept on. This isn't the story
of a housewife dusting the mantle.
It's about the stubborn drive
I have, and you, too. You're
a strange fellow, stretching your
neck into the world. The subject
jumps ahead and leaves you
trudging along, excitement
quickly wilting. Down the road,
the troubled wind, the imprecise
laws of science.
      You pick
your way over debris. You don't
exactly label what you touch. You
register it with a deliberateness
that is more like memory, only
always for the first time.
You don't want to get lost.
You hope for an answer.

You believe you have a mate
who is far out front, but who may
hit a lull. Then you quit
being interested in a subject.
You just want to get through this
with honor. The subject has
disappeared into the meter of
your legs, the heat of the walk.
Even the old problem of religion
has dissolved into walking.

FOR THE INAUGURATION
OF WILLIAM JEFFERSON CLINTON, 1997

Not having been asked to write the inaugural poem,
even though I am from Arkansas, I will take what's here,
the birds at the feeder, not saving the world but only
being it, each kind of bird taking up its career

to fill out some this-or-that of creation on a small scale,
like this poem nobody asked for and few will hear.
Cold birds, eating extra for warmth, finely detailed
to catch the sun. Ridged out in friction-gear,

they jerk from position to position, as if the eye's
first impressions have been caught before the brain
smooths them out. The chickadee clamps a precise
seed and tosses its shell, nothing amazing.

To start up a fanfare would be to see it as specimen,
to deflect one's attention from the exact life performing
its dip, crack, toss. The long beak of the wren
is extended by a thin white stripe traced full-swing

down the head, so the wren seems half beak. I need
to get these lines, delicate as a Chinese painting.
Any poem would quiver with delight, with the chickadee
in it, or wren, but wouldn't want to do anything

about it. That's the hard thing about writing a poem
that's supposed to inspire the country at a crucial time,
that's supposed to hammer like a woodpecker. No one
could hear, with its hammering red, black, white!

It doesn't bode well for the quiet poem, or the insect
inside the bark, or the old tree crumbling to dust
inside itself while the public word *tree* holds it erect.
Still, I think when the bleachers no longer rise august

along Pennsylvania Avenue and the meandering ocean
of confetti has been swept up, it is good to cross a bridge
in your mind, to something earlier, oblivious to emotion,
something like wrens going on inside the language.

V.

SILENCE

YOUR BODY

I could trace everything: where you're
soft, where rough, the taut and slack
of your body I know in the Biblical sense.
I could describe all that, call it metaphor
for the inscrutable, and embarrass you
standing here in your bones, covered
by your black pants and shirt, your successful
tie and suede jacket, professorial, yet
a little rakish — a good and lyrical surface.
I could deconstruct you in front of everybody,
point out your internal contradictions.
Your bald head and hairy chin could
stand for the more complex issues.
I would circle you like the blind man
describing an elephant, making the error
of parts, while you head on out the door
like Wallace Stevens, keeping his
private and cryptic language, never a word
of family, never an allusion to poetry
at the Hartford Insurance Company.
I can hear your body being that quiet,
modest, only decorative enough to affirm
our mutual taste.

        God, I don't know,
I just wanted to say something in *honor*,
and it all looks so confessional.
The body is what teases me, Eliot
in his banker's suit, fingering his spectacles.
Williams returning from rounds,
shirt-sleeves rolled up to reveal hairy
(or not) arms. Bishop, stepping out
of the tub, a few rolls at the stomach,
a little too much weather around the eyes.
Dickinson, pacing her room,

thin white underneath the white—
but secret thigh muscles, powerful
enough, I imagine, to keep all that grace
under pressure.
           Happy, angry, or sad,
I am utterly drawn to this mystery, as if
it were the magnetic center of life, a pole —
oh, and then the Freudians will start in
on me, with their connective tissue of prose!
Memphis the cat is kneading my chest,
press-press, press-press, her eyes blankly
earnest, mouth watering. She doesn't
give a hang if I'm her mother or an iconic
stand-in, it's the flesh she loves under
my sweater, the body of my body of work.

SAMANTHA QUITS GROWING

From ultrasound to ultrasound
she hardly grew at all.
In the old days, we wouldn't
have known, or been able to name

her double-x chromosomes Samantha —
this grandchild, blind seahorse
on its rope swing, making its
debut in Albrecht Dürer stitches.

Not itself, but sound.
Not sound, but sound's thumbprint,
wiggling, silvered, measurable.
Dear Scott — I used to put you

in your playpen, jewel
in a box, to keep you away
from nevermind what. "Take
your vitamin C," I always

say. "Get more exercise,"
as if I could fortify you
against the past, and now
this black-and-white, filled

with imaginings, with
the husbanding of space, with
every test in the book
they did until — who knows

why — your daughter's growth's
picked up again — no Down's,
no MS, just the secret flesh
of human fear exposed

for a couple of months, as if
the soul were on the outside,
hands to its face, small legs
kicking away our attempts at clarity.

ON THE THIRD ANNIVERSARY OF HER DEATH

She would have bent to see the begonias'
    pinkness droop to falling —
        no, that's me —

she would have bent over her *McCall's*
    on the back stoop, while I
        smelled Fall

as I do now under this hickory
    where squirrels have cracked nuts,
        where shells lie

like barnacles on the rain-slick stone
    and I am Darwin studying
        the transmutation of barnacles,

how things change, five days before
    the anniversary of her death
        which I had not

said until now, but which rose
    like steam from these objects,
        including the anemones,

blooming precious few blooms
    on stems too high to support them.
        I am on this cliff

of the year, acorns hitting the tin
    shed behind me like bullets.
        Two hawks circle,

good for them, they have evolved
      their outrageous hymns. They tear
      openly across

the weather with their serrated wings
      like magazine pages ripped
      mid-story.

I WRITE MY MOTHER A POEM

Sometimes I feel her easing further into her grave,
resigned, as always, and I have to come to her rescue.
Like now, when I have so much else to do. Not that

she'd want a poem. She would have been proud, of course,
of all its mystery, involving her, but scared a little.
Her eyes would have filled with tears. It always comes

to that, I don't know why I bother. One gesture
and she's gone down a well of raw feeling, and I'm left
alone again. I avert my eyes, to keep from scaring her.

On her dresser is one of those old glass bottles
of Jergen's Lotion with the black label, a little round
bottle of Mum deodorant, a white plastic tray

with Avon necklaces and earrings, pennies, paper clips,
and a large black coat button. I appear to be very
interested in these objects, even interested in the sun

through the blinds. It falls across her face, and not,
as she changes the bed. She would rather have clean sheets
than my poem, but as long as I don't bother her, she's glad

to know I care. She's talked my father into taking
a drive later, stopping for an A & W root beer.
She is dreaming of foam on the glass, the tray propped

on the car window. And trees, farmhouses, the expanse
of the world as seen from inside the car. It is no
use trying to get her out to watch airplanes

take off, or walk a trail, or hear this poem
and offer anything more than "Isn't that sweet!"
Right now bombs are exploding in Kosovo, students

shot in Colorado, and my mother is wearing a root beer
mustache. Her eyes are unfocused, everything's root beer.
I write root beer, root beer, to make her happy.

EINSTEIN ON MERCER STREET

While a student at the famous Polytechnic at Zurich, Albert Einstein fell in love with the only woman in his class, a Serbian named Mileva Maric, who at first was able to keep up with his mind. They talked physics and declared they'd never settle for a bourgeois life. Their first child, Lieserl, was born before Albert decided they could marry. They either gave her away or she died. Nothing is known about her. They had two other children before their divorce. By this time, Mileva had given up her career and had sunk into a severe depression. A few years later, Einstein won the Nobel Prize and — even though he was married by then to his cousin Elsa — he sent Mileva all the prize money. Twenty-three years later, after Einstein had become a U.S. citizen and a professor at Princeton University, the United States dropped the first atomic bomb on Japan. Einstein had nothing to do directly with the development of the bomb.

I.

Ah, Mileva, it's always you I turn to
        in my thoughts, on my walks down Mercer Street,
lone old lump inside my gray raincoat,

the parabola of my felt hat.
        They keep me like a Kubla Khan
at Princeton. My floating hair they talk of:

His floating hair. Beware! Beware!
        Weave a circle round him thrice.
Reporters flash in my face. Even the bomb,

they claim, was my idea. One marketable God
        of the Intellect, they want. But what they catch —
each shot's a different man.

Put them together, flip quickly,
	and I'm still, I swear, the man you once
thought: a motion picture, a wave, a music,

a disturbance in something else. In you,
	maybe, as you are in me. As if I'd never
left you. A man never loses the woman

he has children with. Even dead.
	It's the hope — what we thought we could be —
that hangs like a moon

over the field of my losses.
	Oh my Dollie, my schnoxel, this is your
Jonzerel-silly-names, fastened to you

by my nerve-endings. We were going to fly
	so far outside the gravity of the bourgeoise,
we would remain all thought, wit, music —

eternal students, the "we" of significant work,
	ein Stein, one stone. Then it all felt like stone.
Now I talk to myself.

II.

Still, somewhere inside the so-called ether,
        I feel you listening — dark, peevish
as always, your intelligence rasping like wire

against mine. Somewhere I'm still
        playing Mozart — in spite of you — half the night,
a fool for him, and Bach, their harmonies,

their unfailing return after infinite variations
        as if the starting point were all time sucked inward,
or some anthropomorphic God were calling

eternity back into this intersection with friends.
        Three Divertimenti: clarinet, piano, me on violin,
the children asleep, you my angry Mileva

curled in shadows, what we each called love, I guess,
        the mathematics we made of our marriage,
against the emptiness.

III.

It appears that the universe bends toward
       itself, a geodesic dome,
two hands, fingertips touching like a person

in thought. If I moved faster than light, I could
       draw the bow back
into the music's mouth, rewind data.

Never allow, for instance, that monstrous
       nuclear heartbreak, *not* my invention,
except for the math I pushed so far

off the edge of reason.
       Where were you? Turning back, giving up
your books, no longer able to follow me.

IV.

Rewinding: Up through swirls of snow, switchback
        turns, precipices, up to Splügen Pass.
You brought opera glasses

and my blue nightshirt. Heads touching as one,
        we studied a snowflake, fractal,
circular. At dawn we sent snowballs down the slopes,

imagined the village below, avalanched.
        Always we had to oppose, to disturb!
The disturbance of pregnancy, then:

our atoms inexorably carrying on.
        I withdrew, as I do, to follow a thought.
Even then I guessed the extremes things could come to:

the snowball chain of split nuclei
        that can start forking through Plutonium,
doubling, quadrupling from one generation

to the next in millionths of a second, releasing
        matter back to vast, primordial energy
you can never put your hands on again.

V.

I thought I was a pacifist. Good work needs
        a certain peace. Ah, then Lieserl —
we agreed, didn't we, what to do

when she was born? So as not to undo
        the future. (Who knew then if we'd ever
marry?) "As what is the child registered?"

 I had to know that, at least. To be a Jew —
        another strike against her. You think
it's peace you've won, but sometimes

it's only quiet, while the violence grows,
        a snowball chain where you can't see.
After the boys were born,

Lieserl would knot and twist
        in my troubled stomach: this cramp.
Every day it feels as if I'm giving birth.

The doctors say drink milk and more milk.
        I wanted peace, so I could think.
This is what I get.

And in Germany, Hitler rose up
        like all my dreams of deformed children,
children sinking in the waves, children lost.

VI.

I note the universe goes from order to disorder,
       yet it remains. With my own eye
I saw a man fall from a building

into a rubbish heap and live.
       The man said he felt no downward pull,
which made me guess that we ride along

inside our own frame, you in your truth,
       me in mine. Why did I have to wear socks,
then, to please you? Because of a universal

fact: mass can't help but bend toward mass.
       I like only shoes, these two boats
that keep me pretty much afloat

by themselves, an elegant sequence, like notes.
       Take Mozart: his perfect symmetry
that gets where it's going. But there has to be

someone outside the music, to listen,
       for it to break the heart with joy.
Who else is left to listen to me, old enemy?

VII.

Since Elsa died, I'm down to
      Chico the dog, *Tinef* my sailboat —
worthless thing, but a pleasure —

and this fame. If I could do it again,
      I swear I'd become a plumber.
The mind can't stand too much pure thought.

It oppresses. You oppress me
      still, my dear, forever brooding.
Things ought not *be* all probability. This

will make you mad: I told Elsa once,
      "If you (meaning her, of course)
were to recite the most beautiful poem,

it would not come close to the mushrooms
      and goose cracklings you cook
for me." Plain things, like sailing.

I can now sail like a swan. I like to be
      carried along, making calculations,
but I admit, truth's not ordinary:

it disappears as soon as you look.
      It's like catching the wind,
trying to make it bend to fit your mind.

VIII.

When I was a schoolboy
      in the Alps in the rain
at the razor-edge of a cliff,

among small black birds,
      when I slipped
in my poor shoes and was barely

caught by a classmate —
      what do you think
would be the mathematics of this?

Since a person freely falling
      could go on forever,
and it's only the sudden embrace

that holds you here,
      or there, how does one
show up at the coordinates

on time? Were we at the right
      place, or wrong,
my little veranda, my Dollie,

my little street urchin? We did
      save each other once, I think,
and once is all there is.

ABOUT THE AUTHOR

Fleda Brown's poems have appeared in *Poetry, The Kenyon Review, The Southern Review, American Poetry Review, The Georgia Review,* and many other journals, and they have been used as texts for several prize-winning musical compositions which have been performed at Eastman School of Music and at Yale University. Her first collection of poems, *Fishing With Blood* (Purdue University Press), won the Great Lakes Colleges Association New Writers Award in 1988.

In 1993, *Do Not Peel the Birches* (Purdue University Press), was chosen by Gerald Stern as winner of the Verna Emery Prize. Her third collection, *The Devil's Child,* was published in 1999 by Carnegie Mellon University Press. She also has a limited edition book of poems and images, *The Eleusinian Mysteries MS,* with Norman Sasowsky (Moment Press, 1992), and a chapbook, *The Earliest House* (Yarrow, 1993). She has written essays on William Dean Howells and Mark Twain, as well as on D.H. Lawrence and other contemporary British writers. She is co-editor with Dennis Jackson of *Critical Essays on D.H. Lawrence,* published in 1988 by G.K. Hall.

She has also written on teaching and writing poetry. Brown grew up in Arkansas, and in 2001 she was awarded that state's premier poetry prize, The Porter Fund Prize for Literary Excellence. She is now professor of English at the University of Delaware, where she directs the Graduate Student Poets in the Schools program. She and her husband, Jerry Beasley, live in Newark, Delaware. She is poet laureate of Delaware.

WHAT, PRAY TELL, IS AN ANHINGA?

Closely related to cormorants, anhingas are found in the Deep South — most commonly in Florida. Our logo depicts an anhinga striking its signature pose, a stance the bird must hold for long stretches of time after each underwater fishing expedition because, lacking oil glands to dry them more quickly, its wings are too soggy to fly. The sinuous anhinga is also known as the snakebird for the way it swims with all but head and neck submerged below the surface of the water.